MW01055075

Painting with Stitches

Sue Dove
Painting with Stitches

Interweave Press
www.interweave.com

To Pom-Pom, for always believing in me.

Text and stitched designs copyright ©2004 Sue Dove
Photography copyright ©2004 David Porteous Editions
Book design and layout copyright ©2004 David Porteous Editions

ISBN: 1-931499-56-X

Interweave Press
201 East Fourth Street
Loveland, Colorado 80537-5655 USA
www.interweave.com

Originally published in 2004 in the U.K. by David Porteous Editions

All rights reserved

Library of Congress Cataloging-in-Publication Data

Dove, Sue.
  Painting with stitches : free-style embroidery by hand / Sue Dove.
    p. cm.
  ISBN 1-931499-56-X
  1. Embroidery--Patterns. I. Title.
  TT771.D65 2004
  746.44'041--dc22
                                                    2003024911

10 9 8 7 6 5 4 3 2 1

Printed in China.

CONTENTS

FOREWORD

WOVEN tapestry was my first love when I began studying textiles. It enabled me to transfer my paintings into textiles and retain the same qualities of imagery, tone, color and scale. Tapestry also had the added bonus of texture. However, after I left college I soon found that without their facilities my output was severely restricted. Thankfully I discovered embroidery, a process that has given me a much greater freedom from technical constraints. I could still develop my pictorial imagery without losing the glorious texture of tapestry.

I not only love threads but also the act of creating a textile, yet I still feel like a painter. I fill piles of sketchbooks with drawings, paintings and collages—playing with color, patterns, materials and imagery. These provide the basis and starting point for my embroideries and paintings. I often use images that surround me—china, flowers, people and animals—reworking them from my imagination and in my own style. An embroidery may be developed by taking areas from a whole number of drawings, collages, oil pastels or photographs.

When I begin stitching, I only draw a very minimal outline onto the canvas because I like my embroideries to evolve and retain a painterly form. I cannot stitch freely if I have to follow a rigid guide. I want the work to grow into itself, slowly, at its own pace.

Embroidery has a long history and importance in our domestic and cultural worlds, from the embroidered garments of priests and warriors to everyday items in the home, using the materials of our physical world to convey our spiritual needs. My embroideries are an integral part of my life—my home, memories, pleasures and inspiration—and they all tell a story of the slow, focused, contented, exquisite joy of stitching with color. I hope you will feel inspired to take up needle and thread and experience this same deep satisfaction.

INTRODUCTION

I have always liked to work in both paint and thread. Painting allows me freedom to move color around while I use narrative to develop images of creatures and figures. The stitched work evolves from these expressions of joy and humor.

Tulips and Fruit *Woven tapestry in embroidery floss. 9 inches x 5½ inches (23cm x 14cm)*

OR me, a day without embroidering is almost as unthinkable as a day without breathing. A certain amount of obsessive addiction is very nearly the only way to produce a volume of work as a hand embroiderer, given the slow nature of the work. It is this slow pace, this contemplative, restful quality to hand embroidery that I love so much. The fact that, armed with a small bag of threads, I can venture anywhere to embroider and frequently do—the beach, bluebell woods, traffic jams, boring meetings, public transport, almost anywhere in fact. It is quite amazing how much you can produce in small "bites." I always work on several pieces at one time, moving back and forth between them. The style, compositions and form of execution then evolve over a period of time and each piece becomes unique. My work has become a culmination of associations between the animate and the inanimate world and how I respond to them.

I started life in textiles as a tapestry weaver, spending three wonderful years at Liverpool School of Art on the textile degree course. It was a splendid time; a free, wide-ranging course, where I left feeling very much an artist as opposed to a designer.

I began to embroider in earnest after my first child was born. Being a compulsive maker, I was looking for something more flexible around babies than painting and tapestry weaving. I started with tent stitch on needlepoint canvas but found it too neat and regular. I soon abandoned this for a more painterly approach, blending colors and imagery with long and short stitches. I later discovered that this was satin stitch.

So began an eighteen-year increasing passion for embroidery, with many projects going on at once

Blue Vase *Woven tapestry in silk, cotton and chenille. 13 inches x 11 inches (33.5cm x 28.5cm)*

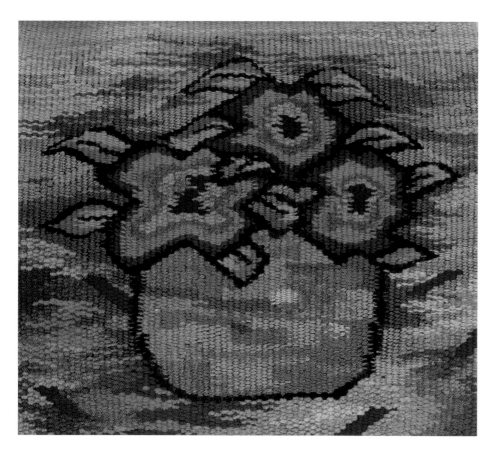

Blue Flowers *(left) Woven tapestry in embroidery floss and chenille.*
9 inches x 10 inches
(23cm x 25.5cm)

Wrapped Flowers *(facing page) Woven tapestry with the stems of the flowers wrapped and a piece of needlepoint tapestry placed behind the stems. The yellow pot has embroidered flowers on its surface.*
8½ inches x 5½ inches (22cm x 14cm)

because of the need to start on new ideas. Lately, I have moved into three-dimensional, completely embroidered pieces, figures and animals that have evolved from my paintings. Over the years I have made small, embroidered brooches, selling them at local galleries and to friends. These have been a good way to promote embroidery, making it accessible and wearable. With my wall pieces, I am constantly in a dilemma as to how to display them, whether to put them behind glass or to leave them completely unframed. It is so easy to lose their tactile quality by turning them into a glazed or framed picture.

I work a lot with collage and oil pastels, both in my sketchbooks and larger finished pieces. These provide the ideas and starting points for my textiles. I also make felt, three-dimensional pieces, often large, with embroidery worked into them. I like to combine these with my tapestry weaving.

Having a studio near St. Ives (a hub for artists and craftspeople in the southwest of England), I am surrounded by art and artists, which is a rousing and constant influence and source of inspiration. I spend a lot of time looking at paintings both in galleries and in books—studying color imagery, movement and pattern, and seeing how artists resolve and display them. I particularly like colorists, Kandinsky, the Fauves, Hundertwasser, Matisse, and the Delaunays. Among other more modern painters who inspire me are Tony O'Malley, Alan Davie, Ken Kiff. I am also interested in Outsider Art (Jean Dubuffet's Art Brut) and Tribal Art, both so original and inspiring.

In 1987, we moved with our three children to Australia. Although I

Dryad 1 *(above) One of a series of hand embroidered three-dimensional Dryad figures.*
Height 8½ inches (21.5cm)

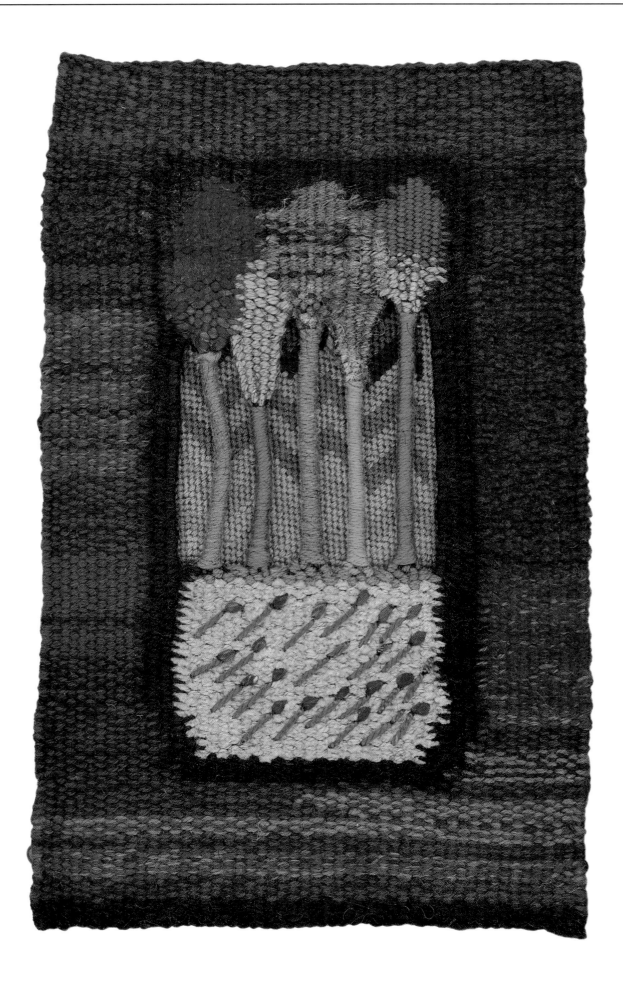

Dove *A hand-embroidered three-dimensional figure. Height 9½ inches (24cm)*

love that country, pangs of homesickness on my part have meant spending our lives between the two countries. This has made a varied and colorful life and proved to be a very stimulating influence on my work. As many will know, there is a thriving, lively textile movement in Australia, helped along by the magazine *Textile Fibre Forum* and their splendid annual Easter forums at Mittagong—a week of sheer unadulterated bliss for anyone remotely interested in textiles. Every other year, Janet De Boer, the editor and organizer, invites overseas artists, many from the U.K., to run workshops. I have found the colors, energy and images of Australia and the exposure to the artworks there, combined with all that happens in Cornwall, a rich and fertile world in which to live and work.

Embroidered Brooches

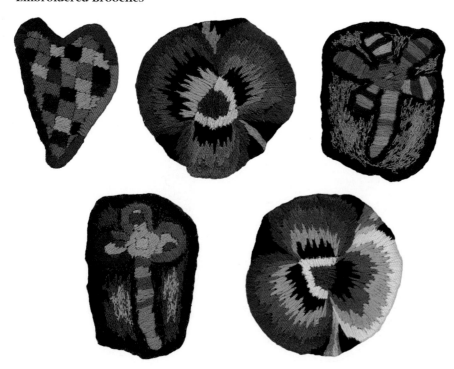

Zig Zag Flowers *(facing page) Shaped woven tapestry with needlepoint behind the stems and a patchwork border embroidered with running and other stitches. 12¼ inches x 10¼ inches (31.5cm x 26.5cm)*

Materials & Techniques

I have always considered whatever materials and techniques I use in my work as merely a vocabulary to express my ideas. In my embroidery I use the most simple and basic approach that anyone can follow.

I AM not obsessive about either techniques or materials. I do not believe there is a "right" or "wrong" way of doing things. It is much more important to find a way of expressing your ideas in such a way that the technique or materials help rather than hinder your creativity. When I first began to embroider, I didn't even know the name of the stitch I was using. All that mattered was that I got the result I wanted. The following are my suggestions because they work for me. You may find other materials better suited to how *you* personally work and how you express *your* ideas. Feel free to break any rules you don't like!

Canvas

I always use needlepoint double-thread canvas, also known as Penelope canvas. Canvas comes in a variety of gauge or mesh sizes and these are specified in either holes or threads per inch (for example, 10 count means 10 holes per inch). I almost always use the 10-count size. Penelope canvas can be purchased in white or antique (brown) shades. I invariably use the antique rather than the white because it is less obvious if it shows between the stitches. Single-thread canvas can be used but my preference is for double-thread because it gives more choice for positioning my stitches. The needle can be inserted through either the large or small holes and this helps to create curved shapes.

I like this canvas because it has a fairly rigid work surface and will handle the weight of the thread without too much distortion. However, there will always be some distortion or movement but I consider that a part of the unique quality of each design. If you are unhappy about the distortion, then the alternative is to work with the material held in an embroidery frame. Using a frame is a slower process because each stitch has to be made in two movements. First the needle is passed entirely through the canvas and

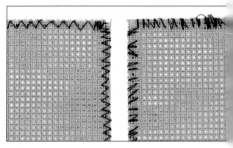

Two pieces of needlepoint canvas showing their edges stitched to prevent the canvas fraying. The one on the right is hand-stitched and the other has been machine zigzagged.

An alternative to needlepoint canvas is ordinary painting canvas or heavyweight fabric. This allows you to decorate your work with fabric paints, if you wish.

If you find it necessary to extend the size of your embroidery, simply sew another piece of canvas to the original piece and stitch over the join.

the thread pulled after it. The needle is then pushed upwards through the canvas and then the thread is pulled through again. If the canvas is not framed, it can be bent slightly so that the needle and thread pass in and out in one movement.

You may wish to experiment with an alternative to canvas and try a heavyweight fabric similar to oil painter's canvas, provided it can handle the weight of the threads without too much distortion.

Needles

I use crewel needles because they have a fine sharp point and larger eyes than ordinary sewing needles which allow me to use thicker thread. I like the fine point because it gives me the opportunity to insert the needle through either the large or small holes of the double-thread canvas.

Thread

The thread I use is stranded cotton floss that is made up of six individual strands. I do not separate the strands but prefer to sew with all six strands, which enables me to cover the canvas more easily. Stranded cotton floss is available in a vast variety of tones and hues so you don't have to compromise on color choice. The strands can, of course, be separated and mixed if you wish. You can even add metallic floss.

Stitches

All my embroideries are stitched using satin or long and short stitches. These simple stitches are perfect for achieving a painterly effect. I always work in one direction, but you can experiment with this. However, it is much more difficult to completely cover the canvas if you do not stitch on a slant. I work the stitches very closely together so

A sample of 10-count Penelope canvas and the basic long and short stitch that I use in my embroideries. Note that most of the stitches are worked diagonally across the canvas.

that they overlap. This gives a rich, sumptuous effect and usually no canvas shows through.

I do not work from a chart because I like to keep the design fluid and allow the embroidery to grow and evolve. A simple outline drawn on the canvas should be a sufficient guide for scale and positioning. The outline drawings included throughout the gallery section of this book are there to

help you but don't follow them slavishly. Allow your own personality and
creativity to take over. Some of my
works have a stitched black outline
and with these I begin by doing all the
black outlines and then filling in the
color interiors. If a work doesn't have
a stitched outline to the shapes, such
as some of my abstract pieces, I start in
the middle of the canvas and work
outwards. I construct figures and creatures in a similar way by starting with
the face and working outwards.

Method

Work diagonally across your canvas so
as to cover it completely. Working
straight up and down will often result
in the canvas showing through. It also
doesn't give the embroidery such a
flowing look to it. Always work your
threads very closely together. I use
stranded cotton floss and I do not ever
separate the individual strands.

Remember to first stitch around
the edges of your piece of canvas to
prevent it from fraying while you
work. You can do this either with the
zigzag stitch on your sewing machine
or overstitch it by hand. This is important as the canvas is loosely woven and
does fray easily. You will also need to
leave a margin of at least one inch
(2.5cm) from the edge of your embroidery to the edge of the canvas.
Obviously on smaller items, such as
brooches, leave a smaller margin. It is
very frustrating if your canvas starts to
fray adjacent to your stitching.

Mounting and Framing

Whether or not to put embroideries
behind glass? Many people feel you
lose much of the tactile quality of the
work, but many of my patrons seem to
prefer it. I have certainly sold more
pieces since I began box-framing my
embroideries. The general opinion is

that it keeps them clean and protected
and they look more "professional."
However, you do need to find a good
picture framer who understands your
work.

Irrespective of whether they are
box-framed or not, I often surround
my embroideries with pieces of fabric,
such as silk dupion. I then stitch ran-
domly with running stitches and a finer
thread, as in *Bird's Eye View* (page 92)
and *Yellow Dog* (page 96). Although
this makes the work much larger, I still
frame them with a surrounding mat
board of approximately 2½ inches
(6.3cm).

Card frames are another option
for mounting your work. Depending
on the size you make them, they can

*The embroideries "Two Vases" (above) and
"Yellow Dog" (facing page) were finished
with fabric "frames." I added more stitches
with finer threads so that the embroidery
flows out to the edges. If you work in this way,
it enables you to create a larger finished
piece and contrast the additional fabrics
with the rich, intensely satin-stitched
embroidery.*

become a major part of your image
with the embroidery a smaller part of
the finished work, as in *Portrait* (page
72) and *Three Spires* (page 102).
Alternatively, mount two or more small
embroideries together. To make a card

work. If your embroidery begins to have a drab, flat appearance, then a strongly contrasting tone should be introduced, either a lighter or darker one. This can liven your work's appearance considerably.

The use of color for me is a very personal means of expression and it gives individuality to my work. Color, as opposed to the design, can be the most powerful element in an embroidery and is crucial to the strength of the whole work.

However, bear in mind that any individual color is always relative and is affected by the adjacent colors, light, texture and form which are all variable factors. Because colors are affected by colors surrounding them, to say that one is brighter or lighter than another is relative. The same color against a darker background looks brighter than it does against one lighter in tone than itself.

Although aware of all this theory, I always feel that I choose my colors instinctively. I am very particular about using the "right" color, and I often undo hours of work if I decide a color is "wrong." Because my embroideries are worked in strong colors, I need a vast range of threads of every hue and tone imaginable, because unlike painting one cannot just "mix" the color required. I do spend a long time looking at and selecting colors, and I love the endless permutations you can create just laying threads next to each other.

Gallery Drawings
The embroideries in the gallery section (pages 46–125) have line drawings that can be used as a guide for marking your canvas. They can easily be enlarged on a photocopier and the percentage enlargement is shown on each drawing.

frame I simply cut a strong piece of card, decorate it with textures and cover the whole thing with layers of tissue paper and glue, working around the opening(s). When dry, I paint it with acrylic paint or oil pastels.

Color
Many books are available on color theory. It can become extremely complex, so I will not attempt to go into great depth on the subject. However, it is useful to have a basic understanding of color usage and terminology. Quite simply there are three *primary colors*—red, blue and yellow. The *secondary colors*, purple, green and orange, are each formed by mixing two of the primaries (red + blue = purple, blue + yellow = green, red + yellow = orange). The three *tertiary colors* are mixtures of the primaries and secondaries and produce colors such as russet, olive and citron.

A *hue* is the color itself, and can be one of the primaries or any of the above mixtures. Black added to a hue produces a *shade* or darker color. White added to a hue produces a *tint* or paler color. The *tone* of a color is the lightness or darkness of that color.

So, every color can be varied either by the addition of another color or by the addition of black or white to produce an infinite number of color and tones. The considered use of tone is essential to the overall success of the color scheme used in a piece of your

BROOCHES make ideal gifts, or even a profitable sideline, if you are able to sell your work through a local gallery or shop. They also make a good starting point to learn the "painting with stitches" technique, and flower subjects are everyone's favorites.

On the facing page I have shown a selection of designs to help fire your imagination.

I first sketched out my design for the brooch using oil pastels. I have used rough textured black paper and the flower centers show this backround paper.

The basic outline of the different shapes has been drawn on the canvas. I then embroidered the flower heads before working outwards to complete the background.

INSPIRATION

I am always inspired by other artists' work, and this often makes a good starting point for developing my own ideas. Much of my work is a reflection of my own environment and my friends and family.

Nᴏᴛ knowing where to start with an idea or design for an embroidery is a problem that is frequently put to me by enthusiastic embroiderers. Although there are many approaches to designing for embroidery, I am offering you a clear and simple method that is successful with embroiderers of all ages and abilities.

You will first need to choose some source material, such as a favorite painting or photograph. When making your choice do make sure that there is enough variety of patterns, shapes and colors in it to produce a selection of interesting ideas. Images that have an overall or repetitive pattern and little color variation are not really suitable for this approach.

To begin you will need to make

The illustrations on these two pages show the progression of an idea from the original oil pastel sketch (above) via a collage (opposite) to the embroidery (left). At each stage I try to develop the idea so that the final embroidery retains the spontaneity of the original idea.

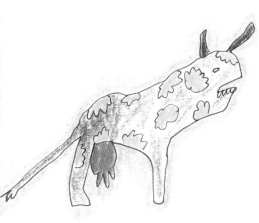

a viewfinder. This is simply a "window" approximately 2½ inches (6.3cm) square cut into a piece of card or thick paper. When you look through this window, it limits the amount of information you can select from your chosen image. However, by moving the viewfinder around it will provide you with lots of image choices.

You could work directly from the section of photo or picture in the viewfinder, but I prefer to personalize it and sketch a colored oil-pastel drawing or painting of the image. You can also further develop the image by making a collage and simply using colored paper torn from old magazines, brochures or junk mail.

Working in collage often helps your design to evolve spontaneously, depending on the colors you find in

your pile of magazines. For example, if you are looking for a solid yellow color and you can only find a yellow with a stripe or pattern on it, then use that instead. Immediately you have added a new personal element to your image. Developing an idea in this way means you start with your original photo or picture but it will change and develop. You can then decide whether or not to use these changes in your embroidery.

Using your artwork as the starting point for your embroidery means that all the decisions about what colors, shapes and patterns to use are all there in your artwork. All you have to do is work them in threads!

You will develop your confidence with collage and drawing as you progress and you will be able to express your own original ideas. We

are surrounded by sources of inspiration that can trigger ideas for shapes, color and textures. The best way to start is to collect together some source materials for visual reference. You can work from anything that inspires you from either natural or man-made objects: shells, flowers, trees, animals, birds, decorated china, textiles, buildings, paintings—the list is endless. Don't forget that ancient and modern cultures offer yet another whole variety of images to inspire you. Part of my "filing system" for these sources is my collection of sketchbooks. I have also built up a collection of photographs, postcards, books and cuttings from magazines.

It is most important to be observant, look diligently at shapes, colors and patterns. Try to record them in a sketchbook. Use media other than just pencil; try oil pastels or collage. The more time you spend on collecting information, the more you increase your powers of observation. As you collect your information, you can make notes on colors you may change, play with patterns, juxtaposing your images and slowly abstracting them from their original look. The more you work in this way, the more confident you will become. As you move farther away from the original source, the more your work becomes personal and develops its own special qualities.

Sketchbook pages. Playing with images of imaginary animals or ideas taken from children's drawings help to develop images that are quirky and individual.

I HAVE always enjoyed playing with colors and seeing how they appear to change when placed next to a different color. These pages are from a sketchbook that I solely devoted to simple color and pattern exercises, page after page. I bought a small sketchbook and a large set of soft colored pencils so that I had a good range of color choices. I filled the sketchbook, trying to do a page a day. In reality it was more often one a week, but I did get there! I often took areas from one page and redeveloped them on the next. I dip into this book to find designs for borders or when I am stuck with a space to fill. This is a good way of building your confidence because you can copy a simple pattern from anything you have around you and play around with it with your pencils.

The following two pages are from one of my other sketchbooks where I developed ideas for my abstract embroideries (see pages 112–125).

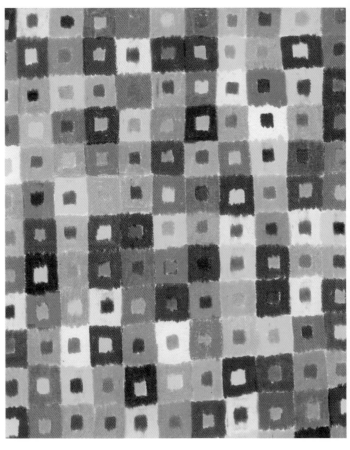

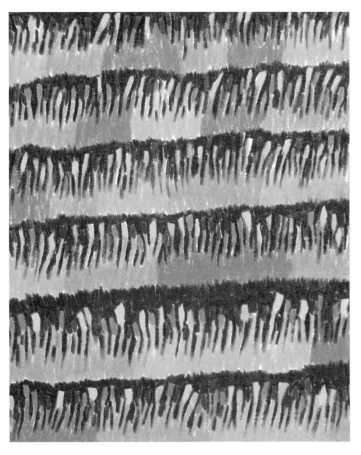

FRIEDENSREICH Hundertwasser is a painter I have admired for many years and his works have given me endless inspiration. His sense of color and pattern make a very rewarding study for any textile artist. My original oil pastel work (above left) echoes the style of Hundertwasser.

In this example of developing an idea I have used my own original painting (above left) as a source but you can just as easily choose any painting. Move your viewfinder around the painting and select an area of the painting that appeals to you. Copy this area using your favorite art materials (colored pencils, paint, or oil pastels).

I next created a collage (above) from my artwork, using old glossy magazine pages as they provide good color ranges. I simply ripped out the shapes and pasted them down, working from my artwork. When working this way you may decide to reproduce the whole image or just part of it. You can, of course, change and move your shapes or colors as you wish.

Remember that your source is only the starting point or guide, and it is up to you how rigidly you stick to it.

The two studies (above) and the two (facing page, below) have been developed by once again placing the viewfinder on the collage and selecting different areas. In each of these four studies I have simplified some shapes and made the colors bolder. You will also see that the scale of the work begins to change.

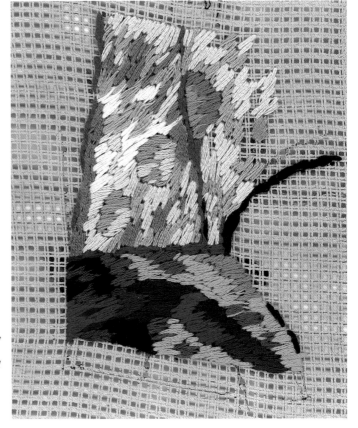

Finally, the embroidery is shown in progress. In interpreting the artwork in stitches I have tried to capture the painterly qualities I achieved in my viewfinder studies where I used oil pastels and colored pencils.

HERE is an alternative way of creating an abstract design without the use of the viewfinder. This time a collage (right) is the starting point. I tore the shapes from an old magazine and I pasted them down leaving plenty of white space around them. You can do this either intuitively or base it on a work from your favorite abstract painter.

Using oil pastels (I prefer Caran d'Ache as they are wonderfully opaque and fluid) I applied the color around the paper shapes to produce rich, vibrant tones.

Cut your artwork into sections. I have cut mine into six rectangular shapes, but you can use any shape or size you like. The best feature about this method is that each shape is an abstract image in its own right.

I have worked one of the smaller rectangular shapes into an abstract style embroidery. You could work one of the shapes or do all of them as a series. Alternatively, if you feel able, work from the whole image instead of cutting it up. Take care in selecting the color of your embroidery threads to reflect the vibrancy of your artwork.

CHICKENS, or "chooks" as I learned to call them in Australia, are wonderful birds to keep. Not only are they often such funny characters but their feathers come in a wide variety of beautiful colors and shapes that are a perfect source of inspiration for painting and stitching.

The embroidery opposite shows something of the rich and colorful textures the feathers provide.

One of my paintings is shown above. I develop ideas in a number of ways and in this instance I began with a detailed painting. This was further expanded as a very loose collage (shown on pages 88–89) and the final embroidered work is shown on the facing page.

I OFTEN draw and paint from a "still life" of fabrics and colorful china, but I first make sure that all the forms complement each other and work together. Flowers feature strongly in my designs, and my favorites are tulips. They are such beautiful flowers —wonderful for painting and easy to interpret in embroidery. The piece shown opposite is worked directly from an oil pastel I made.

First I sketched the outline of the shapes on the canvas with a permanent marker pen. I then embroidered the black outline and finally I stitched in the colors. If you follow this method, it enables you to work out your scale and composition. It also ensures that the design fits your canvas before you spend hours on the details only to find that you cannot fit it all in.

Much of my flower-inspired work has blooms that are contained within pots to create the effect of a still life composition. It is the contrast of delicate petals and the solidity of man-made items which appeals to me, and the challenge of interpreting both "hard" and "soft" textures using similar satin stitches is very rewarding.

Since I was a teenager I have had the collecting bug for china, especially in the 1940s style, with its highly colored strong patterns and imagery. Clarice Cliffe has always been a personal favorite, and I thought that if I cannot own a piece I will paint one!

This piece was worked directly from an oil pastel I created. I stitched the black outline of the forms first and then stitched in the colors.

The embroidery (facing page) is loosely based on the detailed painting on the left. Although flowers may look complicated to stitch, they are really quite simple when broken down into blocks of color. This approach applies equally to all flower interpretations.

PANSIES are invariably so colorful and have such "happy faces" that they have always been a firm favorite. In this embroidery I have combined them with my love of spotted china. Although they may look complicated to stitch, they are really quite simple when broken down into blocks of color. This applies to all flower interpretations. By breaking up the complex form into very simple areas of different colors, it is possible to show the basic form of any flower. When you work on the pot area, avoid covering the area with just one color. Use darker colors for the shaded areas and lighter for the highlighted ones. Dropping in an overall "dot" pattern will also help to create further interest.

Your embroidery will be richer and more interesting if you "play" with the background. This can be quite simple, just by using different tones or introducing patterns that complement the flowers and pots, such as squares behind a spotted pot, or the reverse. Selecting your colors carefully is the answer to achieving a picture that works as a whole. Try some experiments on paper—first with paint or pastels to determine your choice of color, composition and patterns before you start to stitch.

I LOVE all animals, so a great variety of creatures often appear in my work. Additionally, my interest in mythical creatures means that I sometimes merge the real and imaginary and thus create my own species which are adorned with an endless selection of patterns and colors.

I prefer to call them creatures as everyone sees them differently, either as birds or animals—an ambiguity that I like. I make them both in two-dimensional and three-dimensional forms, allowing them to evolve as the work progresses. As this evolution takes place a variety of influences and ideas become entwined and enrich the entire work.

Primitive art and Picasso's distorted images of animals and humans are just some of the influences that are reflected in my works.

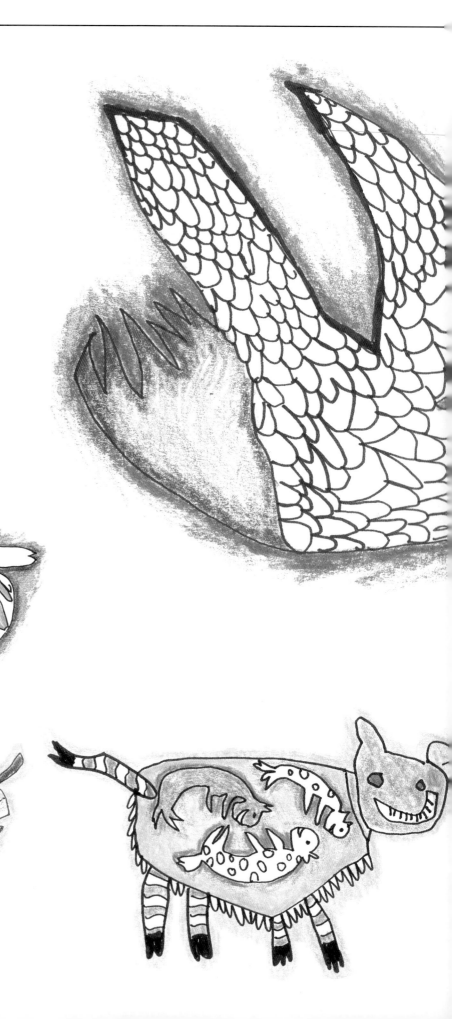

GALLERY

FLOWERS

Flowers bring so much color and joy
into our lives and these pages are a
decorative celebration of the color and
beauty of flowers.

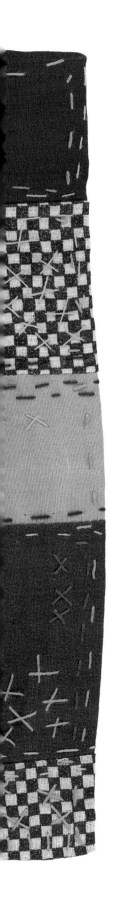

TWO VASES

8¾ inches x 8¾ inches
(22.5cm x 22.5cm)

*Two diminutive pots of flowers sitting
on a checked tablecloth are surrounded
by a generous cotton fabric patchwork
frame, additionally embellished with
finer stitches using fewer strands.*

Enlarge 195%

PANSIES

9 inches x 6¾ inches
(23cm x 17.5cm)

*Pansies are such a beautiful flower
and I have tried to capture some of
their glory in this embroidery. I often
use them as motifs for my brooches
(see page 14).*

Enlarge 160%

FLOWERS IN A BOWL

6½ inches x 5¾ inches
(16.5cm x 15cm)

This is one of my earlier pieces where I experimented with a variety of colored stripes to form a decorative area framing the small bowl of flowers.

Enlarge 135%

TULIPS WITH CHINA

13½ inches x 11 inches
(34.5cm x 28cm)

*I have collected china for many years
and have always admired Clarice
Cliffe's work. This embroidery depicts
a favorite vase filled with tulips.*

Enlarge 240%

ANEMONES

10¼ inches x 11¾ inches
(26cm x 30cm)

*This embroidery made use of pieces of
silk and velvet fabrics combined with
the embroidered areas. This is another
way of "painting with fabric" because
you can more quickly develop an idea
using fabric shapes than stitches.*

Enlarge 250%

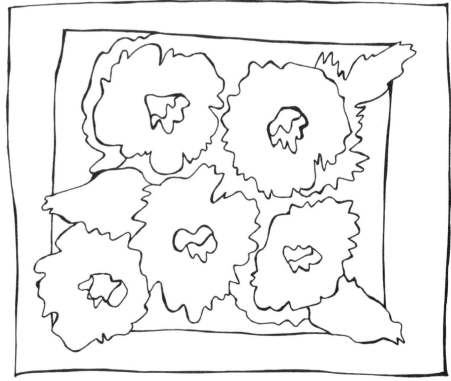

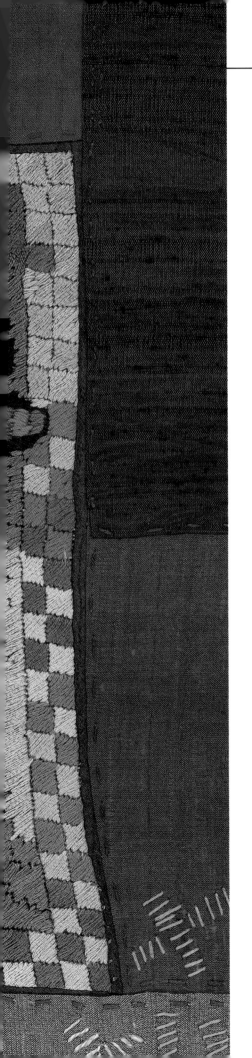

BLUE VASE

12¾ inches x 12¾ inches
(33cm x 33cm)

*The imaginary flowers were treated as
interesting, abstract shapes rather
than a more realistic interpretation.
The same blue vase, another of my
favorites, is depicted on page 11 as a
woven tapestry.*

Enlarge 158%

THREE BLOOMS

5¾ inches x 5¾ inches
(15cm x 15cm)

This is a smaller version of "Blue Vase," the work on the previous page. Here I used machine embroidery to add a finer texture to the background that works well on this scale.

Enlarge 135%

TWO POTS

4¾ inches x 6¼ inches
(12cm x 16cm)

*Again I worked a machine stitch into
the background to add a different
texture, and to contrast it with the
hand stitching of the pots of flowers.*

Enlarge 135%

TULIPS

7¾ inches x 5¾ inches
(20cm x 14.5cm)

*This began as a hand-embroidered
piece but I outlined the flowers with
black machine embroidery. I did this
to simulate a drawn "hatched" outline
that adds a particular dynamism to
the design.*

Enlarge 125%

SPOTTED CHINA JUGS

10 inches x 10 inches
(25.5cm x 25.5cm)

*I have a large collection of spotted
china, some of which is featured in
this embroidery. The background
behind the pots and flowers is a
stitched version of a woven tapestry
that I made a few years ago. The
diagonally striped border helps to
pull the work together.*

Enlarge 215%

TULIPS AND PEAR

11¾ inches x 9¼ inches
(30cm x 24cm)

*This picture was stitched working
directly from my original oil pastel
drawing. I tried to preserve the
vibrancy of the original by using as
many different tones of each color as
in the original oil pastel.*

Enlarge 175%

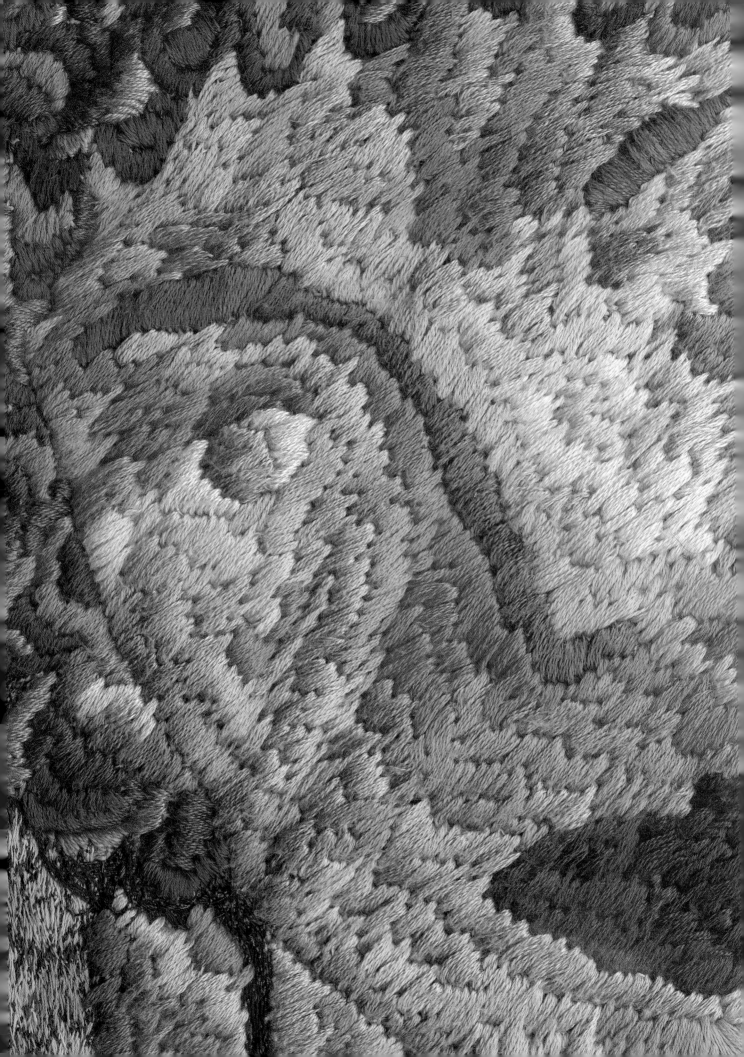

GALLERY

FIGURES

People and their relationships are fascinating. I like to tap in to some of this narrative, using expressive faces and ambiguous situations.

PORTRAIT

Image: 3½ inches x 3 inches
(9cm x 7.5cm)
Frame: 11 inches x 8¼ inches
(28cm x 21cm)

*This small embroidered face is
enhanced by its large decorative
frame. To make the frame, cut a
piece of thick card to shape, leaving
an opening for the embroidery. To
create a three-dimensional effect,
place triangular pieces cut from the
card around the opening. Cover the
whole thing with two or three layers
of tissue paper using glue. When
dry, decorate the frame with paint
and oil pastels.*

Actual size

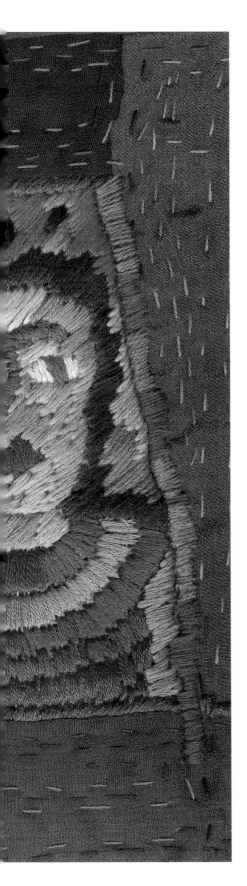

THREE'S COMPANY

7¾ inches x 12¾ inches
(20cm x 33cm)

*The composition was loosely based on
the faces of three of my friends. The
faces have been simplified, but I still
feel that each has its own distinctive
character. The embroidery is finished
with a stitched patchwork surround or
frame.*

Enlarge 275%

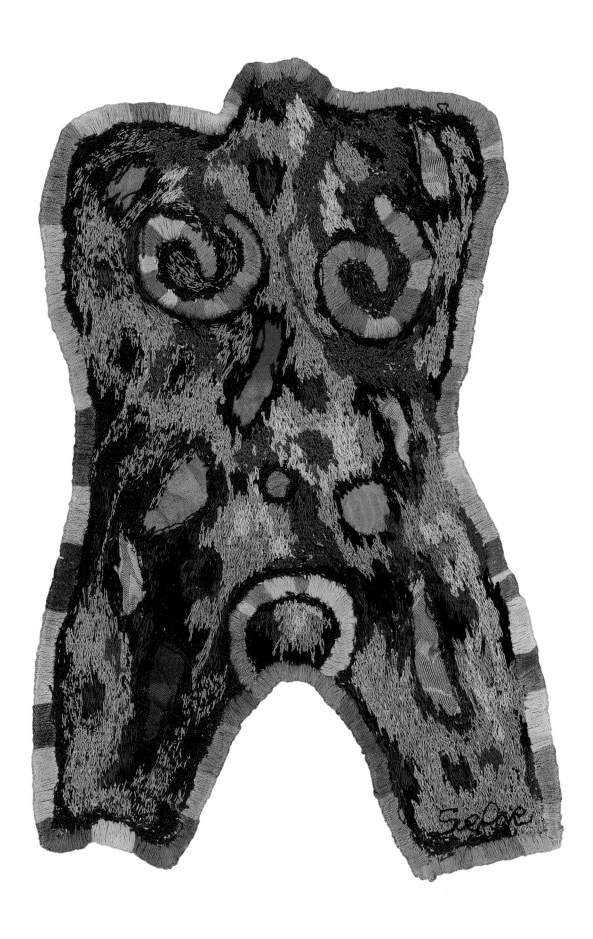

TORSO

7¾ inches x 5½ inches
(20cm x 14cm)

*The torso came from a series of
works dealing with "body image"
issues—a fascinating subject. It is
a mixture of hand and machine
embroidery and includes pieces
of satin and silk fabrics from
my "rag bag."*

Enlarge 135%

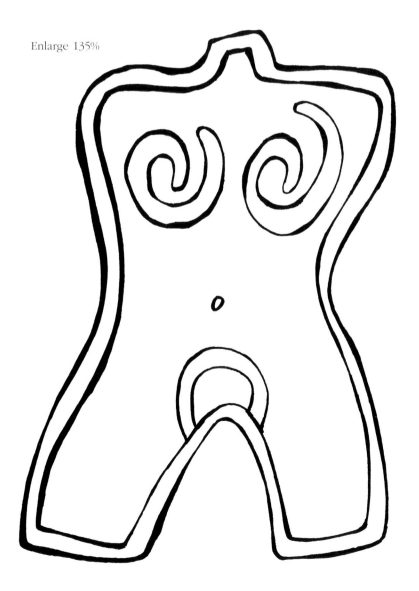

LOVE IN A BOAT

10½ inches x 11¾ inches
(27cm x 30cm)

*This work evolved from a group of
paintings dealing with relationships
and telling stories using dream-like
images. Once again I have used
machine embroidery to add a
different texture.*

Enlarge 213%

FACING IT

11¾ inches x 12½ inches
(30cm x 32cm)

*This piece is largely hand-embroidered
but with a machine-embroidered
background. This combination causes
the handstitching to distort, but this is
an effect that I particularly like. It does
make the presentation of the finished
work challenging!*

Enlarge 280%

WOMEN WILL WAIT

18¼ inches x 19¼ inches
(47cm x 49cm)

*This embroidery depicts four
generations of women and was
inspired by a conversation with some
female friends. One was talking
about a long, agonizing wait for
some medical treatment. It made
me consider how much of our lives
we spend waiting for various
events, dreams or desires.*

Enlarge 415%

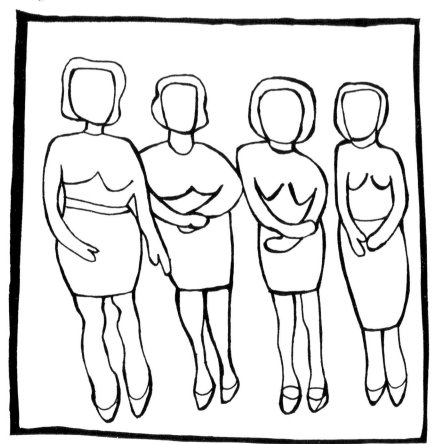

LOOKING FOR TOMORROW

11 inches x 17¼ inches
(28cm x 44cm)

*This narrative piece depicts a woman
with a wistful expression, gazing into
the distance—or perhaps the future.
The melancholy subject contrasts with
the vibrancy of the colors.*

Enlarge 375%

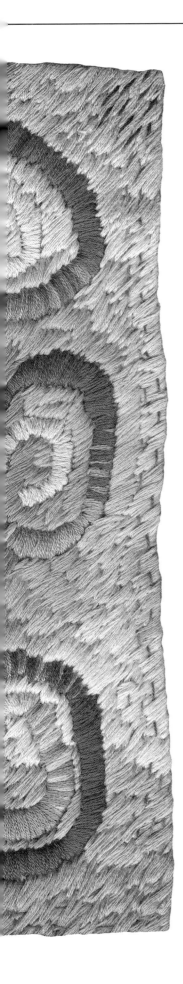

SPIRAL DANCER

11 inches x 12 inches
(28cm x 30.5cm)

*A decorative work celebrating
pure pattern with the spirals in the
background surrounding the dancer.
An Egyptian painting originally
inspired me to design this figure.*

Enlarge 215%

GALLERY

CREATURES

Animals have always been important to me, especially dogs and birds. My creatures are imaginary and evolve from my paintings and drawings.

CHOOKS

10½ inches x 10½ inches
(27cm x 27cm)

*When I raised chickens, I loved their
beautiful flecked feathers and the
individual characters. I have tried to
capture the essence of this in my
embroidery.*

Enlarge 185%

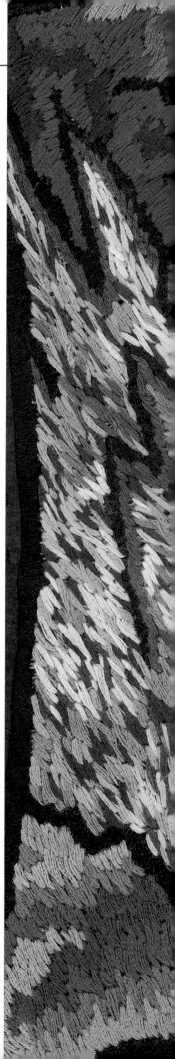

BIRD'S EYE VIEW

21 inches x 21½ inches
(54cm x 55cm)

*This large embroidery includes images
from many of my smaller works—
cabins, creatures and flowers. The
rich tones in the background give the
piece movement and depth. The fabric
frame is made from pieces of colored
silk dupion, using running stitches
to link in with the embroidery. This
fabric frame is not only a way of
presenting the embroidery, but also
for enlarging smaller embroideries.*

Enlarge 340%

WALKING THE DOG

14½ inches x 13½ inches
(37cm x 34.5cm)

*A dog-like creature occupies his
own environment made up of a
rich, patterned background with
tree-like forms.*

Enlarge 180%

YELLOW DOG

9 inches x 9¾ inches
(23cm x 25cm)

*This dog-like image and the one on
the previous page have been used in a
number of my embroideries. In a
sense they have become my
archetypal dogs.*

Enlarge 115%

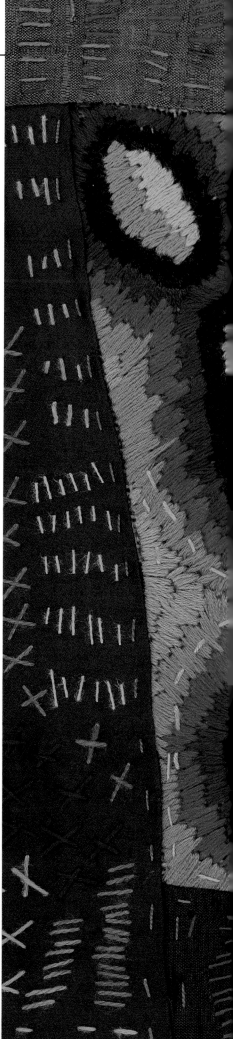

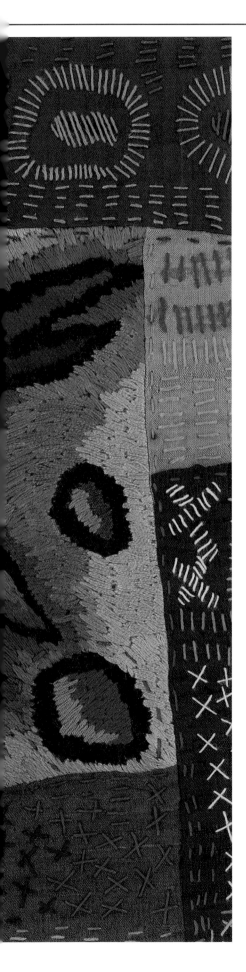

BIRD

9¾ inches x 14¼ inches
(25cm x 36.5cm)

I created this bird from a series of drawings and paintings of different birds, but in its stitched form it has developed its own unique character.

GALLERY

LANDSCAPES

My embroideries usually depict an imaginary landscape, using some recognizable elements but with a very personal and idiosyncratic quality.

THREE SPIRES

Image: 2¼ inches x 2¼ inches
(6cm x 6cm)
Frame: 9¾ inches x 7¾ inches
(25cm x 20cm)

*This small cameo embroidery was
taken from the larger "Tallowland"
(overleaf). The frame is made from
cardboard using a collage of layers of
textured materials, tissue paper and
paint.*

Actual size

TALLOWLAND

8¼ inches x 10¼ inches
(21cm x 26cm)

*This embroidery was developed
from a series of oil pastels inspired
by the paintings of Friedensreich
Hundertwasser. The black outline
adds drama to the colors and gives
them a stained-glass quality.*

Enlarge 210%

BOATS

7¼ inches x 6¼ inches
(19cm x 16cm)

*This embroidery was worked from a
series of paintings and collages of
Cornish harbors. It was inspired by a
photograph of Mousehole Harbour
where the boats are beached close to
the doors of the cottages.*

Enlarge 145%

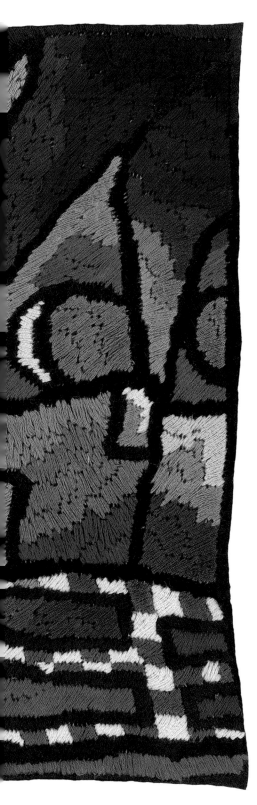

PUMPFIELD ROW

8¼ inches x 10¼ inches
(21cm x 26cm)

*Once again Hundertwasser's paintings
inspired me to produce a series of
oil pastel studies which were later
developed into this embroidery.
Whenever you feel inspired by another
artist, don't follow their work slavishly
(artists' copyright must always be
respected and not infringed)—always
add your own special qualities and
style.*

Enlarge 240%

CORNISH LANDSCAPE

4 inches x 10¼ inches
(10cm x 26cm)

*I am fortunate enough to have a
wonderful view of the Cornish
countryside from my bedroom
window, and it provided the
inspiration for this work. I initially
produced a series of oil pastels and
this embroidery was worked from
one of them.*

Enlarge 145%

GALLERY

ABSTRACTS

In my abstract works I use areas of color against each other and play with their relationships to create movement and pattern.

DOORWAYS

9¼ inches x 8½ inches
(23.5cm x 21.5cm)

The oil pastel on the previous page was
the basis for this work, once again
influenced by Friedensreich
Hundertwasser's art.

Enlarge 180%

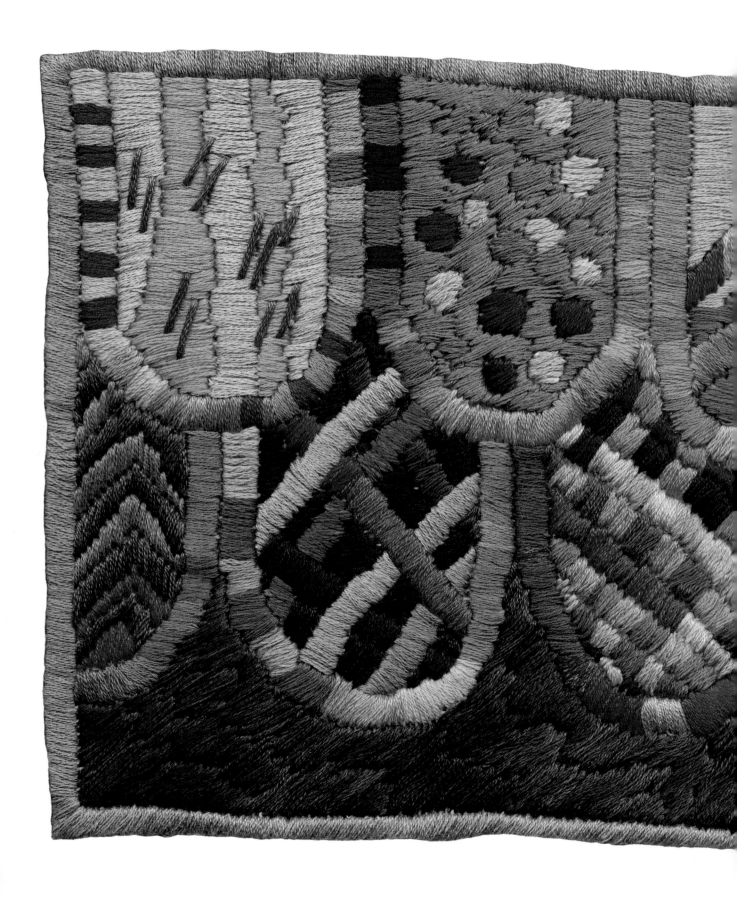

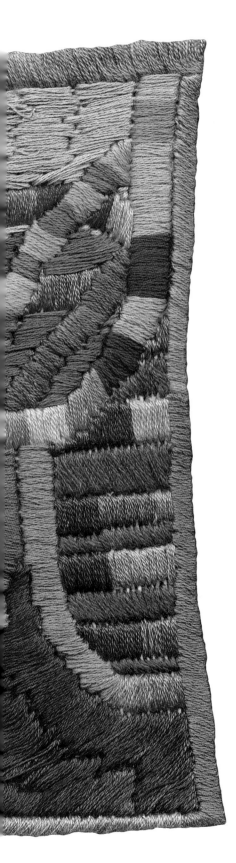

FLAGS

6½ inches x 7½ inches
(16.5cm x 19.5cm)

I was inspired by Indian textiles to create this abstraction of a series of flags, although there are also echoes of medieval heraldic shields evidenced here.

Enlarge 165%

CIRCULAR FORMS

3½ inches x 3 inches
(8cm x 7.5cm)

*As an example of playing with color
and tone, this group of vibrant forms
was stitched from a series of small oil
pastels that were inspired by Wassily
Kandinsky's circle paintings.*

Actual size

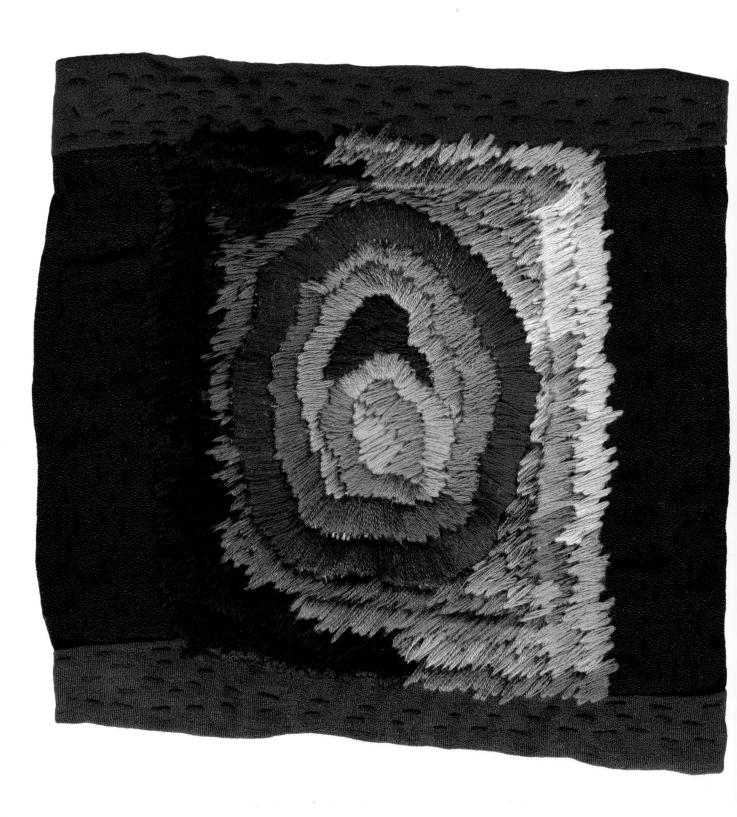

CIRCULAR FORM

5½ inches x 5½ inches
(14cm x 14cm)

*Like the work on the previous
page, this was also inspired by
Kandinsky. The stitch-embellished
patchwork frame echoes the
colors of the embroidery.*

Enlarge 125%

CIRCLES

8¼ inches x 5¾ inches
(21cm x 15cm)

*This work was developed from
a collage where I played with
small blocks of color to create
the rhythmic, circular forms.*

Enlarge 130%

Squares and Spiral

7¼ inches x 7¼ inches
(18.5cm x 18.5cm)

*Many of my embroideries contain
areas drawn from previous
pieces—re-worked elements that
I have thought successful. The
black and white area here has
a powerful effect.*

Enlarge 155%

SUPPLIERS

Oil Pastels

USA

Caran d'Ache of Switzerland, Inc.
38-52, 43rd Street
Long Island City, NY 11101
tel: (718) 483-7500
fax: (718) 482-6700
e-mail: CdAofS@aol.com

Canada

Pierre Belvedere, Inc.
Montreal, Quebec
tel: (514) 286-2880
fax: (514) 286-2890
e-mail: amannheim@pierrebelvedere.com

Culmer Pen Company
Mississauga, Ontario L5L 5R2
tel: (905) 542-0040
fax: (905) 542-1229

Beaconsfield, Quebec H9W 3X9
tel: (514) 630-6931
fax: (514) 426-4993
e-mail: culmer@idirect.com

Canvas and Floss

USA

Coats American Industrial and Crafts
Two Lakepointe Plaza
4135 South Stream Boulevard
Charlotte, North Carolina 28217
tel: (704) 329-5800
fax: (704) 329-5820

Coats and Clark Consumer Services
PO Box 12229
Greenville, SC 29612-0229
tel: (800) 648-1479

The DMC Corporation
South Hackensack Avenue
Port Kearny Building #10F
South Kearny, NJ 07032
tel: (973) 589-0606

Canada

Coats Patons Crafts
1001 Roselawn Avenue
Toronto, Ontario M68 1B8
tel: (416) 782-4481
fax: (416) 785-1370

Colored Pencils

USA

Corporate Headquarters
Sanford
2711 Washington Boulevard
Bellwood, IL 60104
tel: (800) 323-0749

Canada

Sanford Canada
2670 Plymouth Drive
Oakville, Ontario L6H 5R6
tel: (905) 829-5051

BIBLIOGRAPHY

Baal-Teshuva, Jacob. *Chagall*. Taschen, 2003.

Baron, Stanley. *Sonia Delaunay The Life of an Artist*. Thames and Hudson, 1995.

Becks-Malorny, Ulrike. *Wassily Kandinsky 1866–1944: The Journey to Abstraction*. Taschen, 1999.

Bourne, Patrick. *Anne Redpath 1895–1965*. Canongate Books, 1992.

Bowlt, John E. (Editor) & Drutt, Matthew (Editor). *Amazons of the Avant-garde: Alexandra Exter, Natalia Goncharova, Liubov Popova, Olga Rozanova, Varvara Stepanova and Nadezhda Udaltsova*. Royal Academy Publications, 1999, and Guggenheim Museum Publications, 2003.

Britton, Crystal A. *African American Art: The Long Struggle*. Smithmark, 1996.

Caruana, Wally. *Aboriginal Art*. Thames and Hudson World Of Art Series, 1993.

Cohen, Arthur A. *Sonia Delaunay*. Harry N. Abrams Reprint edition, 1988.

Coss, Melinda. *Bloomsbury Needlepoint*. Ebury Press, 1992.

Delaunay, Sonia. *Patterns and Designs in Full Color*. Dover Publications, 1989.

———. *Rhythms and Colours*. Thames and Hudson, 1972.

Düchting, Dr Hajo. *Kandinsky*. Taschen, 1996.

Erben, Walter. *Joan Miró :1893–1983 the Man and His Work*. Taschen, 1998.

Essers, Volkmar. *Matisse*. Taschen, 1996.

Frankenstein, Alfred. *Karel Appel*. Harry N. Abrams, 1980.

Gooding, Mel. *Gillian Ayres*. Lund Humphries, 2001.

———. *Patrick Heron*. Phaidon Press, 1994.

Griffin, Leonard. *Clarice Cliffe— The Bizarre Affair*. Harry N. Abrams, 1988.

Grishin, Sasha. *Garry Shead: The D H Lawrence Paintings*. Craftsman House, 1994.

Gröning, Karl. *Decorated Skin: A World Survey of Body Art*. Thames and Hudson, 2002.

Joan Miró Foundation. *Joan Miró 1893–1983*. Bulfinch, 1993.

Joyce, Paul. *Hockney On Art*. Little, Brown and Company, 2002.

Kandinsky, Wassily. *Concerning the Spiritual in Art*. Dover Publications, 1977.

Keller, Victoria & Young, Clara. *Alberto Morrocco*. Mainstream Publishing Company, 1993.

Klee, Paul. *Paul Klee on Modern Art*. Faber & Faber, 1985.

Lambirth, Andrew. *Ken Kiff*. Thames and Hudson, 2001.

Lindsay, Kenneth C. & Vergo, Peter (Editor). *Kandinsky : Complete Writings on Art*. DaCapo Press, 1994.

Lloyd, Christopher. *Colour For Adventurous Gardeners*. BBC Worldwide, 2001.

Maizels, John. *Raw Creation: Outsider Art and Beyond*. Phaidon Press, 2000.

Marchesseau, Daniel. *Chagall: the Art of Dreams*. Harry N. Abrams, 1998.

Matisse, Henri & Jacobus, John. *Henri Matisse*. Harry N. Abrams, 1985.

McEwen, John. *Paula Rego*. Phaidon Press, 1992.

McKenzie, Janet. *Arthur Boyd: Art and Life*. Thames and Hudson, 2000.

Mink, Janis. *Miró*. Taschen, 1999.

Morley, Simon. *William Scott: Paintings & Drawings*. Merrell Publishers, 1998.

Neret, Gilles. *Matisse*. Taschen, 2002.

O'Malley, Tony & Lynch, Brian (Editor). *Tony O'Malley*. Scolar Press, 1996.

Partsch, Susanna. *Klee*. Taschen, 1993.

Pearce, Barry. *Brett Whiteley: Art And Life*. Art Gallery of New South Wales, 1995.

Poirier, Maurice. *Sean Scully*. Hudson Hills Press, 1990.

Rand, Harry. *Hundertwasser*. Taschen, 1991.

Raw Vision magazine: 4 Issues Per Year 42, Llanvanor Road, London NW2 2AP, UK or 163, Amsterdam Avenue, #203, New York, NY 10023-50001, USA

Restany, Pierre. *Hundertwasser*. Taschen, 2000.

Rifkin, Ned. *Sean Scully: Twenty Years*. Thames and Hudson, 1995.

PURCHASED AT PUBLIC SALE
OUT OF DATE MATERIAL FROM THE SLCLS

Röthel, Hans Konrad. *The Blue Rider*. Praeger Publishers, 1971.

Schmied, Wieland. *Hundertwasser: Kunsthauswien*. Taschen, 2000.

Scully, Sean, Jarauta, Francisco, Zwelte, Armin & Kluser, Bernd. *Sean Scully: Paintings, Pastels, Watercolors, Photographs 1990–2000*. Richter Verlag, 2001.

Tucker, Michael. *Alan Davie*. Lund Humphries, 1992.

Vann, Philip. *Dora Holzhandle*. Lund Humphries, 1997.

Wilkin, Karen. *Georges Braque (Modern Masters)*. Abbeville Press, 1992.